W9-BAT-807

WE
ARE
CANADA

For Rohan and Malcolm,
and those who came before them

Published in 2012 by Read Leaf
www.readleaf.ca

Text © 2012 Rikia Saddy
Illustrations © 2012 Cameron McLellan

CIP Data available from Library and Archives Canada

ISBN 978-1-927018-20-0

We gratefully acknowledge for their financial support of our publishing
program the Canada Council for the Arts, the BC Arts Council, and the
Government of Canada through the Canada Book Fund (CBF).

10 9 8 7 6 5 4 3 2 1

Book design by Pablo Mandel
CircularStudio.com

This book is typeset in Mrs Eaves, a transitional serif typeface designed by Zuzana Licko for Emigre in
1996. It honours Sarah Eaves, the wife of printer and typographer John Baskerville, who completed
his unfinished volumes after his death.

Thanks to my editor Scott Steedman, Cameron McLellan, Dimîter Savoff,
Pablo Mandel, Frank Abbott, Lisa Baroldi, Zahra and Salimah Ebrahim,
Brad Fraser, David Young, Nora and John Vaillant, Cheyanne Turions,
Will Willier, Colleen Curry, Sima Weinsaft Matthes, Suleka Mathew,
Damir Hot, Stephen Irving, Brendan Burke, Denis Walz, May Brown,
Zoiey Cobb, and Mark Kelley.

WE
ARE
CANADA

RIKIA SADDY

READ LEAF

ONCE UPON A TIME, there was a country. Her name was Canada.

She was cold — very, very cold — but she had a fire in her belly.

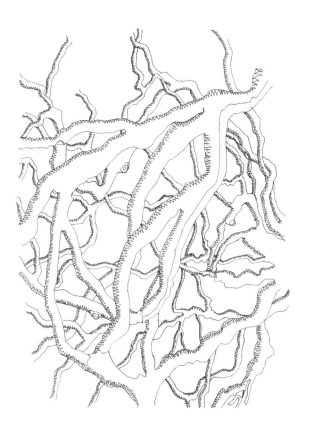

For most of history, she was covered in ice. What wasn't covered in ice was filled with forest. And that's how she rolled, back and forth, ice age to forest to ice age to forest, until so much water was locked up in her ice that ocean levels fell and her first inhabitants walked across a land bridge to Alaska and down the coast, ten thousand years ago.

And the rest is history.

W E WERE TAUGHT the history of Canada was a struggle between the English and the French. In fact, we've been multicultural from the start.

There were hundreds of vibrant cultures across the country in our First Nations. The first European visitors were the Vikings, who landed each year at the tip of Newfoundland in search of fish, wood and pasture for their sheep, about five hundred years before the English or French even set foot on Canada.

It was the Portuguese who named Labrador.

Later, while the French and English were settling central Canada, we had other visitors. In the West, Russians travelled down from Alaska, while the Spanish made their way up the coast from their colonies in Mexico. Americans crossed the border and began settling in the prairies, along with religiously persecuted Europeans.

From the beginning, Canada was a veritable soup of cultures and nationalities. It would turn out to be our greatest strength.

When we tell Canada's history, we work from right to left. It's as though nothing happened in the West until after the French and English worked things out in the middle. But the story that Canada had only two founding peoples is a myth.

Why does that myth endure?

How does a nation that doesn't know its own history survive?

The feeling of being a conquered people lives deep in the hearts of French Canadians. Enter a public building in Quebec and you'll likely find a painting of the battle of the Plains of Abraham. Why would a society memorialize the battle they lost, when they went on to win the next one just a few months later?

The French and the English had more in common than you'd ever know from the stories that were later told to divide and conquer.

Those who came to settle the wilds of Canada shared strength, bravery and allegiance to their kings. Those kings determined how the colonies would evolve.

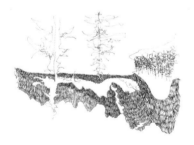

The English colonies accepted everyone and flourished. The French colonies, banned by their king from welcoming anyone who wasn't both French and Catholic, struggled to survive.

This was the first of many times in our history when we discovered that we are stronger in diversity.

We've learned this lesson many times. Our history is filled with the power of newcomers.

The Hutterites, Doukhobors and Mennonites, who came to settle the prairies in return for a promise not to make them fight a war.

Ismailis fleeing Idi Amin and Persians escaping the Shah, who became successful and grateful Canadians.

The Chinese, who built the railways at the rate of three deaths per mile. When the job was over, we said Thank You with a head tax.

Fear can make us forget who we are.

We feared the Acadians and sent them south. We feared Ukrainian, Italian and Japanese Canadians and shipped them to stark internment camps.

We made obscure travel laws to keep East Indians from making the crossing to Canada.

We created residential schools to eliminate aboriginal culture.

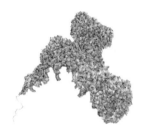

In the Second World War, a million Canadians fought the Nazis, but when a boat of escaping Jews sought our shores, we turned it away. Our immigration policy was "One is too many." Those actual words. That was our Canada's decision.

Dear Reader,

There is a missing "*N*" on page 26. The policy was

"None is too many."

Our sincere apologies.

We take such pride in what we accomplished in the war, how much credit and respect we earned as a nation. We didn't change our immigration policy until it was over.

People learn by making mistakes, and thank-fully, so does Canada.

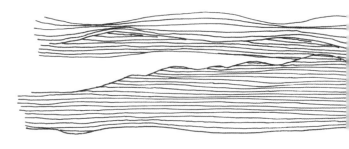

Eventually, when we could no longer look our friends and neighbours in the eye, we decided who we, as a nation, wanted to be.

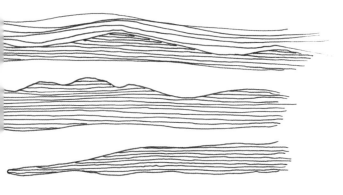

Our shared humanity became more important than our imagined differences.

We became Canada.

How did that happen?

It didn't happen in 1759, when the English conquered the French in battle on the Plains of Abraham, though you may have learned that in school. The English did win that battle, but it did not decide the future of our country.

The next spring, in the Battle of Sainte-Foy, the French trounced the British, leaving them hungry, wounded and in hiding. The French army waited for reinforcements that never came.

Somehow, France had lost her love for Canada. In the popular book *Candide*, Voltaire mocked so much fuss over a "few acres of snow."

Weakened from battle losses in Europe, France had little left to give her colony. The British Navy arrived to fortify her troops and end the Seven Years' War.

At the start of the war, the French had the support of most First Nations and controlled most of North America.

There was still no Canada to speak of. Back when the world was being divided and conquered like a game of Risk, disputes were eventually resolved by kings and diplomats in trade agreements. Canada was no different. Her fate was not sealed until the Treaty of Paris of 1763.

In that meeting, France relinquished her right to Canada in order to hold on to the Caribbean islands of Guadeloupe and Martinique, which were valued for sugar and the spice trade. Britain was given control over Canada, as she already had much of the continent. Look at that date: 1763. The American Revolution would soon weaken Britain's hold on North America, but the point is that France traded Canada.

Little changed for the people of Quebec, who kept their religious, political and social culture. In 1774 the Quebec Act guaranteed the right of Canadiens to practice Catholicism and use French civil law. There was peace.

In fact, by 1812, when the Americans came up to liberate the French from British control (they were on a roll), English, French and First Nation soldiers joined together to beat the invaders back down South.

This is Canada.

We grumble, then we get along.

We built Canada. This was our home, and the only country we knew. We weren't French anymore. Or English. We were Canadian. We were our future.

THERE WERE PEOPLE living in this place long before it was called Canada.

There is a powerful myth in North America that our First Nations just quietly faded away. An equally powerful myth says they were conquered.

Neither is true.

When European settlers first arrived, our First Nations sought out trade. Canada was late to the Bronze Age. Metal tools and weapons were alluring. Our people wanted what the Europeans had to offer.

In return, the Europeans wanted beaver pelts.

Entire First Nation cultures reorganized around the fur trade in order to supply European fashion.

The Europeans didn't just bring guns, shiny buttons, textiles and alcohol. They brought diseases that wiped out thousands.

The First Nations also destroyed each other, in violent battles over access to furs to trade.

Sometimes our common humanity isn't pleasant. This was a time of divide and conquer, and few were spared the desire to get their share.

First Nations played a major role in the creation of Canada. For centuries, they held a powerful position, playing the French off the English for increasing favours.

When France left Canada, the politics shifted, yet models of First Nations governance would go on to become the very foundation of democracy in North America. The First Nations built Canada too.

When the government wanted to settle the West, they considered the fifty thousand people already living there. The Hudson Bay Company had sold their land to the Canadian government, but it didn't come with clear title. Bureaucrats were dispatched to settle the land claims.

The First Nations agreed to surrender all rights to the land, forever, in exchange for exclusive reserves of land, cash payments to each band member, and continued royalties. They negotiated more in each treaty, after speaking with each other and learning what to ask for. They had seen what had happened in the United States, and wanted to prevent a bloodbath.

Buffalo were disappearing. Other cultures were arriving. The First Nations tried to get what was best for their people. No one knew if it would turn out to be best a hundred years later.

Again Canada was traded.

The Indian Act and the Quebec Act reflected the wisdom of the day.

This is how Canada happens. Negotiate, compromise, trade, repeat. There isn't a culture in Canada that hasn't had to adapt to changing circumstance.

But there isn't a culture in the world that hasn't had to adapt to changing circumstance.

Canada had a head start. We've been negotiating and compromising, trading and accommodating, for a thousand years, maybe more.

SOMETIMES, AS A MULTICULTURAL NATION, there's been a lot to accommodate. In 1847, a hundred thousand Irish arrived fleeing famine. They were poor. Dirt poor. They arrived in "coffin ships" bringing new diseases that wreaked havoc in port towns. And in a region delicately balanced between English Protestants and French Catholics, the arrival of so many Catholics from the British Isles upset the social structure.

If Canada could survive the arrival of the Irish, it could survive anything. Now, of course, they are pillars of our society.

We forget how hated and resented they were when they arrived.

That's how Canada works. We knew we needed immigration to grow across this enormous country, and so with every new arrival, we moved over and made room. We adjusted our expectations of what Canada is. We baked a cake for our neighbours and knocked on their door.

Sometimes those who've been here longest complain that Canada is changing too much.

They forget that they were once the wave that changed Canada.

EACH ONE OF US has a story to tell of how we got here.

On my mother's side, my grandmother Dora Morin was French Canadian. My grandfather Lee Tingley was English Canadian. The entire Tingley family has been documented in six volumes of genealogy tracing the path from Samuel Tingley, who arrived in the 1600s. I'm in the sixth book.

They may have thought of themselves as French and English, but by the time my grandparents were born, our country was such a mix of cultures that there was no such thing as *pure laine* anymore.

Both of my father's parents arrived from Lebanon. My great-grandmother brought my young grandmother Rikia for a visit, leaving her elder daughter at home — a decision that left her crying for days. When the ship's officer took one look at her red eyes, he suspected a horrible disease, and wouldn't let them board.

They caught the next boat, via Mexico, but arrived during the Mexican Revolution and were forced to disembark. They were stranded for five years until it was safe to travel and join family in Canada.

War broke out in Lebanon, and despite a lifetime of searching, my great-grandmother never found her elder daughter. A visit turned into a lifetime, and she cried herself to sleep for the rest of her life.

These are the people we talk about when we speak of immigrants.

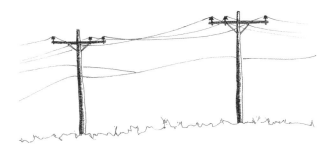

We forget about lives changed, families torn apart, sacrifices made, all in hopes of a better life for the next generation.

We forget how much building a country hurts.

PEOPLE FROM EVERY COUNTRY in the world have built Canada. That's why Canada is always changing. For centuries it has left us without a clear identity.

We wanted to be like countries with a single language, food, and culture.

Now, in an age of globalization and mass migration and collapsing borders and dizzying technological advances, every country in the world is trying to deal with change. And they're asking Canada how we manage to get along.

It's easy when you have a history like ours.

If we, the people of the world, are going to survive, we're going to have to work together. And who knows how to do that?

Canada.

We can't be divided and we can't be conquered.
We are Canada.